O'REILLY®

Strata
Making Data Work

Learn how data into decisions.

T0260885

From startups to the Fortune 500, smart companies are betting on data-driven insight, seizing the opportunities that are emerging from the convergence of four powerful trends:

- New methods of collecting, managing, and analyzing data

- Cloud computing that offers inexpensive storage and flexible, on-demand computing power for massive data sets

- Visualization techniques that turn complex data into images that tell a compelling story

- Tools that make the power of data available to anyone

Get control over big data and turn it into insight with O'Reilly's Strata offerings. Find the inspiration and information to create new products or revive existing ones, understand customer behavior, and get the data edge.

O'REILLY®

Visit oreilly.com/data to learn more.

Scaling MongoDB

Scaling MongoDB

Kristina Chodorow

Beijing · Cambridge · Farnham · Köln · Sebastopol · Tokyo

Scaling MongoDB

by Kristina Chodorow

Copyright © 2011 Kristina Chodorow. All rights reserved.
Printed in the United States of America.

Published by O'Reilly Media, Inc., 1005 Gravenstein Highway North, Sebastopol, CA 95472.

O'Reilly books may be purchased for educational, business, or sales promotional use. Online editions are also available for most titles (*http://my.safaribooksonline.com*). For more information, contact our corporate/institutional sales department: (800) 998-9938 or *corporate@oreilly.com*.

Editor: Mike Loukides	**Cover Designer:** Karen Montgomery
Production Editor: Holly Bauer	**Interior Designer:** David Futato
Proofreader: Holly Bauer	**Illustrator:** Robert Romano

Printing History:

February 2011:   First Edition.

ISBN: 978-1-449-30321-1

[LSI]   [2011-02-22]

1298397997

Table of Contents

Preface

This text is for MongoDB users who are interested in sharding. It is a comprehensive look at how to set up and use a cluster.

This is *not* an introduction to MongoDB; I assume that you understand what a document, collection, and database are, how to read and write data, what an index is (*http://www.mongodb.org/display/DOCS/Indexes*), and how and why to set up a replica set (*http://www.mongodb.org/display/DOCS/Replica+Sets*).

If you are not familiar with MongoDB, it's easy to learn. There are a number of books on MongoDB (*http://www.mongodb.org/display/DOCS/Books*), including *MongoDB: The Definitive Guide* (*http://oreilly.com/catalog/9781449381585/*) from this author. You can also check out the online documentation (*http://www.mongodb.org/display/DOCS/Home*).

Conventions Used in This Book

The following typographical conventions are used in this book:

Italic
: Indicates new terms, URLs, email addresses, filenames, and file extensions.

`Constant width`
: Used for program listings, as well as within paragraphs to refer to program elements such as variable or function names, databases, data types, environment variables, statements, and keywords.

`Constant width bold`
: Shows commands or other text that should be typed literally by the user.

`Constant width italic`
: Shows text that should be replaced with user-supplied values or by values determined by context.

This icon signifies a tip, suggestion, or general note.

 This icon indicates a warning or caution.

Using Code Examples

This book is here to help you get your job done. In general, you may use the code in this book in your programs and documentation. You do not need to contact us for permission unless you're reproducing a significant portion of the code. For example, writing a program that uses several chunks of code from this book does not require permission. Selling or distributing a CD-ROM of examples from O'Reilly books does require permission. Answering a question by citing this book and quoting example code does not require permission. Incorporating a significant amount of example code from this book into your product's documentation does require permission.

We appreciate, but do not require, attribution. An attribution usually includes the title, author, publisher, and ISBN. For example: "*Scaling MongoDB* by Kristina Chodorow (O'Reilly). Copyright 2011 Kristina Chodorow, 978-1-449-30321-1."

If you feel your use of code examples falls outside fair use or the permission given above, feel free to contact us at *permissions@oreilly.com*.

Safari® Books Online

 Safari Books Online is an on-demand digital library that lets you easily search over 7,500 technology and creative reference books and videos to find the answers you need quickly.

With a subscription, you can read any page and watch any video from our library online. Read books on your cell phone and mobile devices. Access new titles before they are available for print, and get exclusive access to manuscripts in development and post feedback for the authors. Copy and paste code samples, organize your favorites, download chapters, bookmark key sections, create notes, print out pages, and benefit from tons of other time-saving features.

O'Reilly Media has uploaded this book to the Safari Books Online service. To have full digital access to this book and others on similar topics from O'Reilly and other publishers, sign up for free at *http://my.safaribooksonline.com*.

How to Contact Us

Please address comments and questions concerning this book to the publisher:

> O'Reilly Media, Inc.
> 1005 Gravenstein Highway North
> Sebastopol, CA 95472
> 800-998-9938 (in the United States or Canada)
> 707-829-0515 (international or local)
> 707-829-0104 (fax)

We have a web page for this book, where we list errata, examples, and any additional information. You can access this page at:

> *http://oreilly.com/catalog/9781449303211*

To comment or ask technical questions about this book, send email to:

> *bookquestions@oreilly.com*

For more information about our books, courses, conferences, and news, see our website at *http://www.oreilly.com*.

Find us on Facebook: *http://facebook.com/oreilly*

Follow us on Twitter: *http://twitter.com/oreillymedia*

Watch us on YouTube: *http://www.youtube.com/oreillymedia*

CHAPTER 1

Welcome to Distributed Computing!

In the *Terminator* movies, an artificial intelligence called Skynet wages war on humans, chugging along for decades creating robots and killing off humanity. This is the dream of most ops people—not to destroy humanity, but to build a distributed system that will work long-term without relying on people carrying pagers. Skynet is still a pipe dream, unfortunately, because distributed systems are very difficult, both to design well and to keep running.

A single database server has a couple of basic states: it's either up or down. If you add another machine and divide your data between the two, you now have some sort of dependency between the servers. How does it affect one machine if the other goes down? Can your application handle either (or both) machines going down? What if the two machines are up, but can't communicate? What if they can communicate, but only very, very, slowly?

As you add more nodes, these problems just become more numerous and complex: what happens if entire parts of your cluster can't communicate with other parts? What happens if one subset of machines crashes? What happens if you lose an entire data center? Suddenly, even taking a backup becomes difficult: how do you take a consistent snapshot of many terabytes of data across dozens of machines without freezing out the application trying to use the data?

If you can get away with a single server, it is much simpler. However, if you want to store a large volume of data or access it at a rate higher than a single server can handle, you'll need to set up a cluster. On the plus side, MongoDB tries to take care of a lot of the issues listed above. Keep in mind that this isn't as simple as setting up a single *mongod* (then again, what is?). This book shows you how to set up a robust cluster and what to expect every step of the way.

What Is Sharding?

Sharding is the method MongoDB uses to split a large collection across several servers (called a *cluster*). While sharding has roots in relational database partitioning, it is (like most aspects of MongoDB) very different.

The biggest difference between any partitioning schemes you've probably used and MongoDB is that MongoDB does almost everything automatically. Once you tell MongoDB to distribute data, it will take care of keeping your data balanced between servers. You have to tell MongoDB to add new servers to the cluster, but once you do, MongoDB takes care of making sure that they get an even amount of the data, too.

Sharding is designed to fulfill three simple goals:

Make the cluster "invisible."

> We want an application to have no idea that what it's talking to is anything other than a single, vanilla *mongod*.
>
> To accomplish this, MongoDB comes with a special routing process called *mongos*. *mongos* sits in front of your cluster and looks like an ordinary *mongod* server to anything that connects to it. It forwards requests to the correct server or servers in the cluster, then assembles their responses and sends them back to the client. This makes it so that, in general, a client does not need to know that they're talking to a cluster rather than a single server.
>
> There are a couple of exceptions to this abstraction when the nature of a cluster forces it. These are covered in Chapter 4.

Make the cluster always available for reads and writes.

> A cluster can't guarantee it'll always be available (what if the power goes out everywhere?), but within reasonable parameters, there should never be a time when users can't read or write data. The cluster should allow as many nodes as possible to fail before its functionality noticeably degrades.
>
> MongoDB ensures maximum uptime in a couple different ways. Every part of a cluster can and should have at least some redundant processes running on other machines (optimally in other data centers) so that if one process/machine/data center goes down, the other ones can immediately (and automatically) pick up the slack and keep going.
>
> There is also the question of what to do when data is being migrated from one machine to another, which is actually a very interesting and difficult problem: how do you provide continuous and consistent access to data while it's in transit? We've come up with some clever solutions to this, but it's a bit beyond the scope of this book. However, under the covers, MongoDB is doing some pretty nifty tricks.

Let the cluster grow easily

> As your system needs more space or resources, you should be able to add them.

MongoDB allows you to add as much capacity as you need as you need it. Adding (and removing) capacity is covered further in Chapter 3.

These goals have some consequences: a cluster should be easy to use (as easy to use as a single node) and easy to administrate (otherwise adding a new shard would not be easy). MongoDB lets your application grow—easily, robustly, and naturally—as far as it needs to.

CHAPTER 2

Understanding Sharding

To set up, administrate, or debug a cluster, you have to understand the basic scheme of how sharding works. This chapter covers the basics so that you can reason about what's going on.

Splitting Up Data

A *shard* is one or more servers in a cluster that are responsible for some subset of the data. For instance, if we had a cluster that contained 1,000,000 documents representing a website's users, one shard might contain information about 200,000 of the users.

A shard can consist of many servers. If there is more than one server in a shard, each server has an identical copy of the subset of data (Figure 2-1). In production, a shard will usually be a replica set.

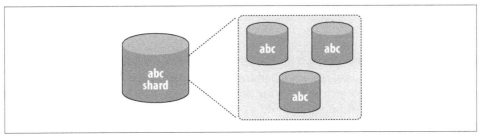

Figure 2-1. A shard contains some subset of the data. If a shard contains more than one server, each server has a complete copy of the data.

To evenly distribute data across shards, MongoDB moves subsets of the data from shard to shard. It figures out which subsets to move based on a key that you choose. For example, we might choose to split up a collection of users based on the *username* field. MongoDB uses range-based splitting; that is, data is split into chunks of given ranges —e.g., ["a", "f").

Throughout this text, I'll use standard range notation (*http://en.wikipedia.org/wiki/Interval_(mathematics)#Excluding_the_endpoints*) to describe ranges. "[" and "]" denote inclusive bounds and "(" and ")" denote exclusive bounds. Thus, the four possible ranges are:

x is in (a, b)
    If there exists an *x* such that $a < x < b$
x is in (a, b]
    If there exists an *x* such that $a < x \leq b$
x is in [a, b)
    If there exists an *x* such that $a \leq x < b$
x is in [a, b]
    If there exists an *x* such that $a \leq x \leq b$

MongoDB's sharding uses *[a, b)* for almost all of its ranges, so that's mostly what you'll see. This range can be expressed as "from and including *a*, up to but not including *b*."

For example, say we have a range of username *["a", "f")*. Then "a", "charlie", and "ez-bake" could be in the set, because, using string comparison, "a" ≤ "a" < "charlie" < "ez-bake" < "f".

The range includes everything *up to but not including* "f". Thus, "ez-bake" could be in the set, but "f" could not.

Distributing Data

MongoDB uses a somewhat non-intuitive method of partitioning data. To understand why it does this, we'll start by using the naïve method and figure out a better way from the problems we run into.

One range per shard

The simplest way to distribute data across shards is for each shard to be responsible for a single range of data. So, if we had four shards, we might have a setup like Figure 2-2. In this example, we will assume that all usernames start with a letter between "a" and "z", which can be represented as *["a", "{")*. "{" is the character after "z" in ASCII.

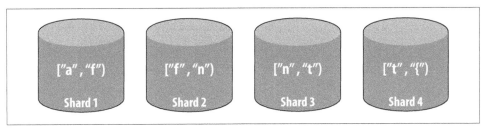

Figure 2-2. Four shards with ranges ["a", "f"), ["f", "n"), ["n", "t"), and ["t", "{")

This is a nice, easy-to-understand system for sharding, but it becomes inconvenient in a large or busy system. It's easiest to see why by working through what would happen.

Suppose a lot of users start registering names starting with ["a", "f"). This will make Shard 1 larger, so we'll take some of its documents and move them to Shard 2. We can adjust the ranges so that Shard 1 is (say) ["a", "c") and Shard 2 is ["c", "n") (see Figure 2-3).

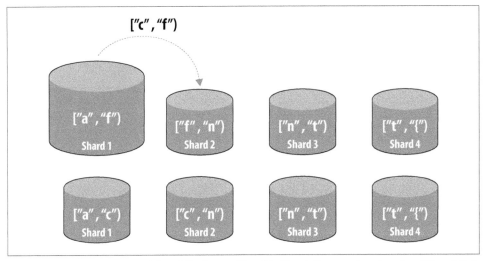

Figure 2-3. Migrating some of Shard 1's data to Shard 2. Shard 1's range is reduced and Shard 2's is expanded.

Everything seems okay so far, but what if Shard 2 is getting overloaded, too? Suppose Shard 1 and Shard 2 have 500GB of data each and Shard 3 and Shard 4 only have 300GB each. Given this sharding scheme, we end up with a cascade of copies: we'd have to move 100GB from shard 1 to Shard 2, then 200GB from shard 2 to shard 3, then 100GB from shard 3 to shard 4, for a total of 400GB moved (Figure 2-4). That's a lot of extra data moved considering that all movement has to cascade across the cluster.

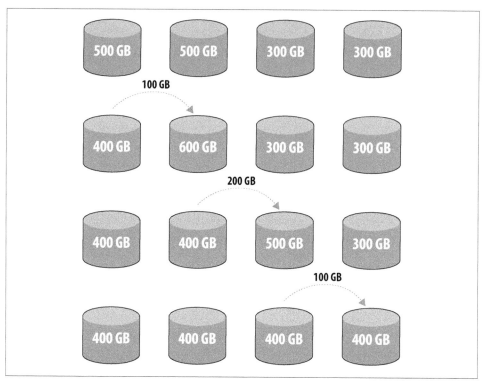

Figure 2-4. Using a single range per shard creates a cascade effect: data has to be moved to the server "next to" it, even if that does not improve the balance

How about adding a new shard? Let's say this cluster keeps working and eventually we end up having 500GB per shard and we add a new shard. Now we have to move 400GB from Shard 4 to Shard 5, 300GB from Shard 3 to Shard 4, 200GB from Shard 2 to Shard 3, 100GB from Shard 1 to Shard 2 (Figure 2-5). That's 1TB of data moved!

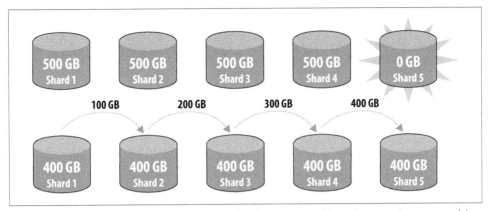

Figure 2-5. Adding a new server and balancing the cluster. We could cut down on the amount of data transferred by adding the new server to the "middle" (between Shard 2 and Shard 3), but it would still require 600GB of data transfer.

This cascade situation just gets worse and worse as the number of shards and amount of data grows. Thus, MongoDB *does not* distribute data this way. Instead, each shard contains multiple ranges.

Multi-range shards

Let's consider the situation pictured in Figure 2-4 again, where Shard 1 and Shard 2 have 500GB and Shard 3 and Shard 4 have 300GB. This time, we'll allow each shard to contain multiple chunk ranges.

This allows us to divide Shard 1's data into two ranges: one of 400GB (say *["a", "d")*) and one of 100GB (*["d", "f")*). Then, we'll do the same on Shard 2, ending up with *["f", "j")* and *["j", "n")*. Now, we can migrate 100GB (*["d", "f")*) from Shard 1 to Shard 3 and all of the documents in the *["j", "n")* range from Shard 2 to Shard 4 (see Figure 2-6). A range of data is called a *chunk*. When we split a chunk's range into two ranges, it becomes two chunks.

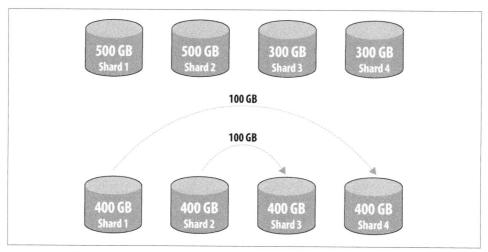

Figure 2-6. Allowing multiple, non-consecutive ranges in a shard allows us to pick and choose data and to move it anywhere

Now there are 400GB of data on each shard and only 200GB of data had to be moved.

If we add a new shard, MongoDB can skim 100GB off of the top of each shard and move these chunks to the new shard, allowing the new shard to get 400GB of data by moving the bare minimum: only 400GB of data (Figure 2-7).

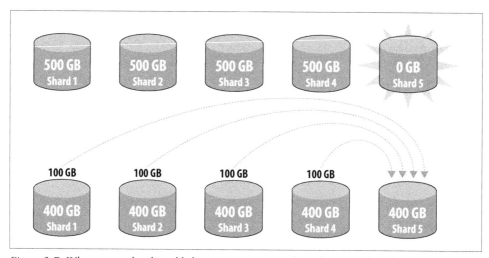

Figure 2-7. When a new shard is added, everyone can contribute data to it directly

This is how MongoDB distributes data between shards. As a chunk gets bigger, MongoDB will automatically split it into two smaller chunks. If the shards become unbalanced, chunks will be migrated to correct the imbalance.

How Chunks Are Created

When you decide to distribute data, you have to choose a key to use for chunk ranges (we've been using `username` above). This key is called a *shard key* and can be any field or combination of fields. (We'll go over how to choose the shard key and the actual commands to shard a collection in Chapter 3.)

Example

Suppose our collection had documents that looked like this (*_ids* omitted):

```
{"username" : "paul", "age" : 23}
{"username" : "simon", "age" : 17}
{"username" : "widdly", "age" : 16}
{"username" : "scuds", "age" : 95}
{"username" : "grill", "age" : 18}
{"username" : "flavored", "age" : 55}
{"username" : "bertango", "age" : 73}
{"username" : "wooster", "age" : 33}
```

If we choose the *age* field as a shard key and end up with a chunk range *[15, 26)*, the chunk would contain the following documents:

```
{"username" : "paul", "age" : 23}
{"username" : "simon", "age" : 17}
{"username" : "widdly", "age" : 16}
{"username" : "grill", "age" : 18}
```

As you can see, all of the documents in this chunk have their *age* value in the chunk's range.

Sharding collections

When you first shard a collection, MongoDB creates a single chunk for whatever data is in the collection. This chunk has a range of *(-∞, ∞)*, where -∞ is the smallest value MongoDB can represent (also called `$minKey`) and ∞ is the largest (also called `$maxKey`).

 If you shard a collection containing a lot of data, MongoDB will immediately split this initial chunk into smaller chunks.

The collection in the example above is too small to actually trigger a split, so you'd end up with a single chunk—*(-∞, ∞)*—until you inserted more data. However, for the purposes of demonstration, let's pretend that this was enough data.

MongoDB would split the initial chunk *(-∞, ∞)* into two chunks around the midpoint of the existing data's range. So, if approximately half of the documents had a an *age* field less than 15 and half were greater than 15, MongoDB might choose 15. Then we'd end up with two chunks: *(-∞, 15), [15, ∞)* (Figure 2-8). If we continued to insert data

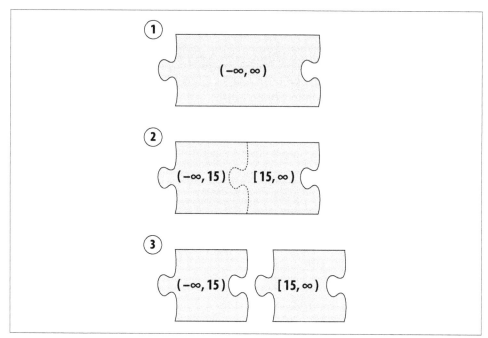

Figure 2-8. A chunk splitting into two chunks

into the *[15, ∞)* chunk, it could be split again, into, say, *[15, 26)* and *[26, ∞)*. So now we have three chunks in this collection: *(-∞, 15)*, *[15, 26)*, and *[26, ∞)*. As we insert more data, MongoDB will continue to split existing chunks to create new ones.

You can have a chunk with a single value as its range (e.g., only users with the username "paul"), but every chunk's range must be distinct (you cannot have two chunks with the range *["a", "f")*). You also cannot have overlapping chunks; each chunk's range must exactly meet the next chunk's range. So, if you split a chunk with the range *[4, 8)*, you could end up with *[4, 6)* and *[6, 8)* because together, they fully cover the original chunk's range. You could not have *[4, 5)* and *[6, 8)* because then your collection is missing everything in *[5, 6)*. You could not have *[4, 6)* and *[5, 8)* because then chunks would overlap. Each document must belong to one and only one chunk.

As MongoDB does not enforce any sort of schema, you might be wondering: where is a document placed if it doesn't have a value for the shard key? MongoDB won't actually allow you to insert documents that are missing the shard key (although using null for the value is fine). You also cannot change the value of a shard key (with, for example, a $set). The only way to give a document a new shard key is to remove the document, change the shard key's value on the client side, and reinsert it.

What if you use strings for some documents and numbers for others? It works fine, as there is a strict ordering between types in MongoDB. If you insert a string (or an array, boolean, null, etc.) in the *age* field, MongoDB would sort it according to its type. The ordering of types is:

null < numbers < strings < objects < arrays < binary data < ObjectIds < booleans < dates < regular expressions

Within a type, orderings are as you'd probably expect: 2 < 4, "a" < "z".

In the first example given, chunks are hundreds of gigabytes in size, but in a real system, chunks are only 64MB by default. This is because moving data is expensive: it takes a lot of time, uses system resources, and can add a significant amount of network traffic. You don't want your application to grind to a halt while MongoDB shuffles data in the background; in fact, if a chunk gets too big, MongoDB will refuse to move it at all. You don't want chunks to be too small, either, because each chunk has a little bit of administrative overhead to requests (so you don't want to have to keep track of zillions of them). It turns out that 64MB is the sweet spot between portability and minimal overhead.

 A chunk is a logical concept, not a physical reality. The documents in a chunk are not physically contiguous on disk or grouped in any way. They may be scattered at random throughout a collection. A document belongs in a chunk if and only if its shard key value is in that chunk's range.

Balancing

If there are multiple shards available, MongoDB will start migrating data to other shards once you have a sufficient number of chunks. This migration is called *balancing* and is performed by a process called the *balancer*.

The balancer moves chunks from one shard to another. The nice thing about the balancer is that it's automatic—you don't have to worry about keeping your data even across shards because it's done for you. This is also the downside: it's automatic, so if you don't like the way it's balancing things, tough luck. If you decide you don't want a certain chunk on Shard 3, you can manually move it to Shard 2, but the balancer will probably just pick it up and move it back to Shard 3. Your only options are to either re-shard the collection or turn off balancing.

As of this writing, the balancer's algorithm isn't terribly intelligent. It moves chunks based on the overall size of the shard and calls it a day. It will become more advanced in the (near) future.

The goal of the balancer is not only to keep the data evenly distributed but also to minimize the amount of data transferred. Thus, it takes a lot to trigger the balancer. For a balancing round to occur, a shard must have at least nine more chunks than the least-populous shard. At that point, chunks will be migrated off of the crowded shard until it is even with the rest of the shards.

The reason the balancer isn't very aggressive is that MongoDB wants to avoid sending the same data back and forth. If the balancer balanced out any tiny difference, it could constantly waste resources: Shard 1 would have two chunks more than Shard 2, so it would send Shard 2 one chunk. Then a few writes would go to Shard 2, and Shard 2 would end up with two more chunks than Shard 1 and send the original chunk right back (Figure 2-9). By waiting for a more severe imbalance, MongoDB can minimize pointless data transfers. Keep in mind that nine chunks is not even that much of an imbalance—it is less than 2GB of data.

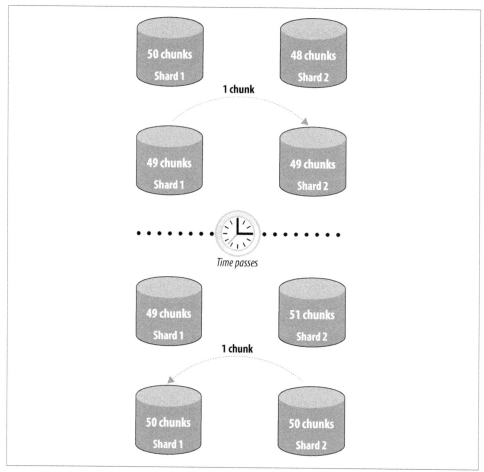

Figure 2-9. If every slight imbalance is corrected, a lot of data will end up moving unnecessarily

The Psychopathology of Everyday Balancing

Most users want to prove to themselves that sharding works by watching their data move, which creates a problem: the amount of data it takes to trigger a balancing round is larger than most people realize.

Let's say I'm just playing with sharding, so I write a shell script to insert half a million documents into a sharded collection.

```
> for (i=0; i<500000; i++) {
    db.foo.insert({"_id" : i, "x" : 1,"y" : 2, "z" : i, "date" : new Date(),
      "foo" : "bar"});
}
```

After half a million documents, I should see some data flying around, right? Wrong. If I take a look at the database stats, I still have a ways to go (some fields have been omitted for clarity):

```
> db.stats()
{
    "raw" : {
        "ubuntu:27017" : {
            /* shard stats */
        },
        "ubuntu:27018" : {
            /* shard stats */
        }
    },
    "objects" : 500008,
    "avgObjSize" : 79.99937600998383,
    "dataSize" : 40000328,
    "storageSize" : 69082624,
    "ok" : 1
}
```

If you look at *dataSize*, you can see that I have 40,000,328 bytes of data, which is roughly equivalent to 40MB. That's not even a chunk. That's not even a quarter of a chunk! To actually see data move, I would need to insert 2GB, which is 25 million of these documents, or 50 times as much data as I am currently inserting.

When people start sharding, they want to see their data moving around. It's human nature. However, in a production system, you don't want a lot of migration because it's a very expensive operation. So, on the one hand, we have the very human desire to see migrations actually happen. On the other hand, we have the fact that sharding won't work very well if it isn't irritatingly slow to human eyes.

What MongoDB did was to let users specify `--chunkSize N`, where `N` is the chunk size that you want in megabytes. If you're just trying out sharding and messing around, you can set `--chunkSize 1` and see your data migrating after a couple of megabytes of inserts.

On changing chunk size

Chunk size can be changed by starting with --chunkSize *N* or modifying the *config.settings* collection and restarting everything. However, unless you're trying out the 1MB chunk size for fun, *don't mess with the chunk size.*

I guarantee that, whatever you're trying to fix, fiddling with chunk size is not going to solve the root problem. It's a tempting knob to play with, but don't. Leave chunk size alone unless you want to play around with --chunkSize 1.

mongos

mongos is the interaction point between users and the cluster. Its job is to hide all of the gooey internals of sharding and present a clean, single-server interface to the user (you). There are a few cracks in this veneer, which are discussed in Chapter 4, but *mongos* mostly lets you treat a cluster as a single server.

When you use a cluster, you connect to a *mongos* and issue all reads and writes to that *mongos*. You should never have to access the shards directly (although you can if you want).

mongos forwards all user requests to the appropriate shards. If a user inserts a document, *mongos* looks at the document's shard key, looks at the chunks, and sends the document to the shard holding the correct chunk.

For example, say we insert {"foo" : "bar"} and we're sharding on foo. *mongos* looks at the chunks available and sees that there is a chunk with the range *["a", "c")*, which is the chunk that should contain "bar". This chunk lives on Shard 2, so *mongos* sends the insert message to Shard 2 (see Figure 2-10).

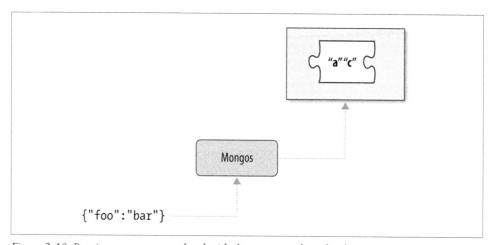

Figure 2-10. Routing a request to a shard with the corresponding chunk

If a query involves the shard key, *mongos* can use the same process it did to do the insert and find the correct shard (or shards) to send the query to. This is called a *targeted query* because it only targets shards that may have the data we're looking for. If it knows we're looking for {"foo" : "bar"}, there's no sense in querying a shard that only contains shard key values greater than "bar".

If the query does not contain the shard key, *mongos* must send the query to all of the shards. These can be less efficient than targeted queries, but isn't necessarily. A "spewed" query that accesses a few indexed documents in RAM will perform much better than a targeted query that has to access data from disk across many shards (a targeted query could hit every shard, too).

The Config Servers

mongos processes don't actually store any data persistently, so the configuration of a cluster is held on special *mongods* called *config servers*. Config servers hold the definitive information about the cluster for everyone's access (shards, *mongos* processes, and system administrators).

For a chunk migration to succeed, all of the configuration servers have to be up. If one of them goes down, all currently occurring migrations will revert themselves and stop until you get a full set of config servers up again. If any config servers go down, your cluster's configuration cannot change.

The Anatomy of a Cluster

A MongoDB cluster basically consists of three types of processes: the shards for actually storing data, the mongos processes for routing requests to the correct data, and the config servers, for keeping track of the cluster's state (Figure 2-11 and Figure 2-12).

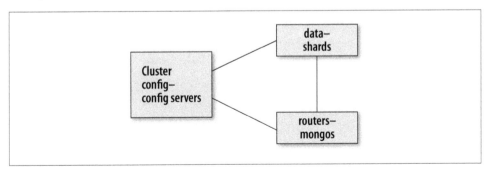

Figure 2-11. Three components of a cluster.

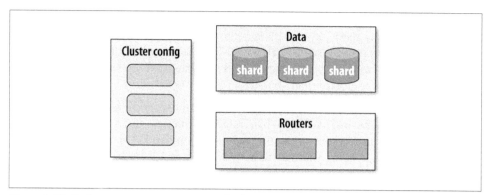

Figure 2-12. Each component can contain multiple processes.

Each of the components above is not "a machine." *mongos* processes are usually run on appservers. Config servers, for all their importance, are pretty lightweight and can basically be run on any machine available. Each shard usually consists of multiple machines, as that's where the data actually lives.

CHAPTER 3

Setting Up a Cluster

Choosing a Shard Key

Choosing a good shard key is absolutely critical. If you choose a bad shard key, it can break your application immediately or when you have heavy traffic, or it can lurk in wait and break your application at a random time.

On the other hand, if you choose a good shard key, MongoDB will just do the right thing as you get more traffic and add more servers, for as long as your application is up.

As you learned in the last chapter, a shard key determines how your data will be distributed across your cluster. Thus, you want a shard key that distributes reads and writes, but that also keeps the data you're using together. These can seem like contradictory goals, but it can often be accomplished.

First we'll go over a couple of bad shard key choices and find out why they're bad, then we'll come up with a couple of better ones. There is also a good page on the MongoDB wiki on choosing a shard key (*http://www.mongodb.org/display/DOCS/Choosing+a +Shard+Key*).

Low-Cardinality Shard Key

Some people don't really trust or understand how MongoDB automatically distributes data, so they think something along the lines of, "I have four shards, so I will use a field with four possible values for my shard key." This is a really, really bad idea.

Let's look at what happens.

Suppose we have an application that stores user information. Each document has a *continent* field, which is where the user is located. Its value can be "Africa", "Antarctica", "Asia", "Australia", "Europe", "North America", or "South America". We decide to shard on this key because we have a data center on each continent (okay, maybe not Antarctica) and we want to server people's data from their "local" data center.

The collection starts off with one chunk—$(-\infty, \infty)$—on a shard in some data center. All your inserts and reads go to that one chunk. Once that chunk gets big enough, it'll split into two chunks with ranges $(-\infty, "Europe")$ and $["Europe", \infty)$. All of the documents from Africa, Antarctica, Asia, or Australia go into the first chunk and all of the documents from Europe, North America, or South America will go into the second chunk. As you add more documents, eventually you'll end up with seven chunks (Figure 3-1):

- $(-\infty, "Antarctica")$
- $["Antarctica", "Asia")$
- $["Asia", "Australia")$
- $["Australia", "Europe")$
- $["Europe", "North America")$
- $["North America", "South America")$
- $["South America", \infty)$

Figure 3-1. One shard per continent

Now what?

MongoDB can't split these chunks any further! The chunks will just keep getting bigger and bigger. This is fine for a while, but what happens when you start running out of space on your servers? There's nothing you can do, aside from getting a bigger hard disk.

This choice of shard key is called a *low-cardinality shard key*, because there are a limited number of shard key values. If you choose a shard key with low cardinality, you will end up with large, unmovable, unsplittable chunks that will make your life miserable.

If you are doing this because you want to manually distribute your data, do not use MongoDB's built-in sharding. You'll be fighting it all the way. However, you can certainly manually shard your collections, write your own router, and route reads and writes to whichever server(s) you'd like. It's just easier to choose a good shard key and let MongoDB do it for you.

Keys that this rule applies to

This rule applies to any key that has a finite number of values. Keep in mind that, if a key has *N* values in a collection, you can only have *N* chunks and, therefore, *N* shards.

If you are tempted to use low-cardinality shard key because you query on that field a lot, use a compound shard key (a shard key with two fields) and make sure that the second field has lots of different values MongoDB can use for splitting.

Exceptions to the rule

If a collection has a lifetime (e.g., you're creating a new collection each week and you know that, in a single week, you won't get near the capacity of any of your shards), you could choose this as a key.

Data center awareness

This example is not just about choosing a low-cardinality shard key, but also about trying to hack data-center awareness into MongoDB's sharding. Sharding does not yet support data center awareness. If you're interested in this, you can watch/vote for the relevant bug (*http://jira.mongodb.org/browse/SERVER-992*).

The problem with hacking it together yourself is that it isn't very extensible. What happens if your application is big in Japan? Now you want to add a second shard to handle Asia.

How are you going to migrate data over? You can't move a chunk once it's more than a few gigabytes in size, and you can't split the chunk because there is only one shard key value in the whole chunk. You can't just update all of the documents to use a more unique value because you can't update a shard key value. You could remove each document, change the shard key's value, and resave it, but that is not a swift operation for a large database.

The best you can do is start inserting "Asia, Japan" instead of just "Asia". Then you will have old documents that should be "Asia, Japan" but are just "Asia" and then your application logic will have to support both. Also, once you start having finer-grained chunks, there's no guarantee MongoDB will put them where you want (unless you turn off the balancer and do everything manually).

Data-center awareness is very important for large applications and it's a high priority for MongoDB developers. Choosing a low-cardinality shard key is not a good solution for the interim.

Ascending Shard Key

Reading data from RAM is faster than reading data from disk, so the goal is to have as much data as possible accessed in RAM. Thus, we want a shard key that keeps data together if it will be accessed together. For most applications, recent data is accessed more than older data, so people will often try to use something like a timestamp or ObjectId field for a shard key. This does not work as well as they expect it to.

Let's say we have a Twitter-like service where each document contains a short message, who sent it, and when it was sent. We shard on when it was sent, in seconds since the epoch.

We start out with one chunk: $(-\infty, \infty)$, as always. All the inserts go to this shard until it splits into something like $(-\infty, 1294516901), [1294516901, \infty)$. Now, we split chunks at their midpoint, so when we split the chunk, the current timestamp is probably well after 1294516901. This means that all inserts will be going to the second chunk—nothing will be hitting the first anymore. Once the second chunk fills up, it'll be split up into $[1294516901, 1294930163), [1294930163, \infty)$. But now the time will be after 1294930163, so everything will be added to the $[1294930163, \infty)$ chunk. This pattern continues: everything will always be added to the "last" chunk, meaning everything will be added to one shard.

This shard key gives you a single, undistributable hot spot.

Keys that this rule applies to

This rule applies to anything ascending; it doesn't have to be a timestamp. This includes `ObjectId`s, dates, auto-incrementing primary keys (imported from other databases, possibly). If the key's values trend towards infinity, you will have this problem.

Exceptions to the rule

Basically, this shard key is always a bad idea because it guarantees you'll have a hotspot. If you have low traffic so that a single shard can handle almost all reads and writes, this could work. Of course, if you get a traffic spike or become more popular, it would stop working and be difficult to fix.

Don't use an ascending shard key unless you're sure you know what you're doing. There are better shard keys—this one should be avoided.

Random Shard Key

Sometimes, in an effort to avoid a hotspot, people choose a field with random values to shard by. This will work fine at first, but as you get more data, it can become slower and slower.

Let's say we're storing thumbnail photos in a sharded collection. Each document contains the binary data for the photo, an MD5 hash of the binary data, a description, the date it was taken, and who took it. We decide to shard on the MD5 hash.

As our collection grows, we end up with a pretty even number of chunks evenly distributed across our shards. So far so good. Now, let's say we're pretty busy and a chunk on Shard 2 fills up and splits. The configuration server notices that Shard 2 has 10 more chunks than Shard 1 and decides it should even things out. MongoDB now has to load a random five chunks' worth of data into memory and send it to Shard 1. This is data that wouldn't have been in memory ordinarily, because it's a completely random order of data. So, now MongoDB is going to be putting a lot more pressure on RAM and there's going to be a lot of disk IO going on (which is always slow).

You must have an index on the key you shard by, so if you choose a randomly-valued key that you don't query by, you're basically "wasting" an index. Every additional index makes writes slower, so it's important to keep the number of indexes as low as possible.

Good Shard Keys

What we really want is something that takes into account our access patterns. If our application is regularly accessing 25GB of data, we'd like to have all splits and migrates happen in the 25GB of data, not access data in a random pattern that must constantly copy new data from disk to memory.

So, we want to choose a shard key with nice data locality, but not so local that we end up with a hot spot.

Coarsely ascending key + search key

Many applications access new data more often than older data, so we want data to be roughly ordered by date, but also distributed evenly. This keeps the data we're reading and writing in memory, but distributes the load across the cluster.

We can accomplish this with a compound shard key—something like {coarselyAscend ing : 1, search : 1}. The coarselyAscending key should have between a few dozen and a few hundred chunks per value and the search key should be something that the application commonly queries by.

For example, let's say we have an analytics application where our users regularly access the last month worth of data; we want to keep that data handy. We'll shard on {month : 1, user : 1}. *month* is a coarsely ascending field, which means that every month it has a new, increasing value. *user* is a good second field because we'll often be querying for a certain user's data.

We'll start out with our one chunk, which now has a compound range: ((-∞,-∞), (∞, ∞)). As it fills up, we split the chunk into two chunks, something like ((-∞, -∞), ("2011-04", "susan")) and [("2011-04", "susan"), (∞, ∞)). Now, assuming it's still April ("2011-04"), the writes will be evenly distributed between the two chunks. All users with usernames less than "susan" will be put on the first chunk and all users with usernames greater than "susan" will be put on the second chunk.

As the data continues to grow, this continues to work. Subsequent chunks created in April will be moved to different shards, so reads and writes will be balanced across the cluster. In May, we start creating chunks with *"2011-05"* in their bounds. When June rolls around, we aren't accessing the data from *"04-2011"* chunks anymore, so these chunks can quietly drop out of memory and stop taking up resources. We might want to look at them again for historical reasons, but they should never need to be split or migrated (the problem we ran into with random indexes).

FAQ

Why not just use {ascendingKey : 1} as the shard key?
> This was covered in "Ascending Shard Key" and, if you combine it with a rough-grained ascending key, it can also create giant, unsplittable chunks.

Can search be an ascending field, too?
> No. If it is, the shard key will degenerate into an ascending key and you'll have the same hotspot problems a vanilla ascending key gives you.

So what should search be?
> Hopefully, the *search* field can be something useful your application can use for querying, possibly user info (as in the example above), a filename field, a GUID, etc. It should be a fairly randomly distributed non-ascending key with decent cardinality.

The general case

We can generalize this to a formula for shard keys:

```
{coarseLocality : 1, search : 1}
```

coarseLocality is whatever locality you want for your data. *search* is a common search on your data.

This key is not the only possible shard key and it won't work well for everything. However, it's a good way to start thinking about how to choose a shard key, even if you do not ultimately use it.

What shard key should I use?

Not knowing your application, I can't really tell you. Choosing a good shard key should take some work. Before you choose one, think about the answers to these questions:

- What do writes look like? What is the shape and size of the documents you're inserting?
- How much data is the system writing per hour? Per day? Peak?
- What fields are random, and which ones are increasing?
- What do reads look like? What data are people accessing?
- How much data is the system reading per hour? Per day? Peak?
- Is the data indexed? Should it be indexed?
- How much data is there, total?

There may be other patterns that you find in your data—use them! Before you shard, you should get to know your data very well.

Sharding a New Collection

Once you have selected a shard key, you are ready to shard your data.

Quick Start

If you're looking to set up a cluster to play around with as fast as possible, you can set one up in a minute or two using the mongo-snippets (*https://github.com/mongodb/mongo-snippets*) repository on Github. It's a little lacking in documentation, but this repository is basically a collection of useful scripts for users. Of particular interest is *simple-setup.py*, which automatically starts, configures, and populates a cluster (locally).

To run this script, you'll need to have the MongoDB Python driver. If you do not have it installed, you can install it (on *NIX systems) by running:

```
$ sudo easy_install pymongo
```

Once Pymongo is installed, download the *mongo-snippets* repository and run the following command:

```
$ python sharding/simple-setup.py --path=/path/to/your/mongodb/binaries
```

There are a number of other options available—run `python sharding/simple-setup.py --help` to see them. This script is a bit finicky, so make sure to use the full path (e.g., /home/user/mongo-install, not ~/mongo-install).

simple-setup.py starts up a *mongos* on *localhost:27017*, so you can connect to it with the shell to play around.

If you are interested in setting up a serious-business cluster, read on.

Config Servers

You can run either one or three configuration servers. We'll be using three config servers, as that's what you should do whenever you're in production.

> "One or three" is a weird and somewhat arbitrary restriction, but the rationale is that one is good for testing, and three is good for production. Two is more than people would want to test with and not enough for production.
>
> You can't run an arbitrary number because their interactions are complex, and the programming and logic of what to do if N out of M config servers are down is difficult. MongoDB probably will support any number of config servers in the future, but it's not an immediate priority.

Setting up configuration servers is pretty boring because they're just vanilla *mongod* instances. The only important thing to note when setting up config servers is that you want some of them up all of the time, so try to put them in separate failure domains.

Let's say we have three data centers: one in New York, one in San Francisco, and one on the moon. We start up one config server in each center.

```
$ ssh ny-01
ny-01$ mongod

$ ssh sf-01
sf-01$ mongod

$ ssh moon-01
moon-01$ mongod
```

That's it!

You might notice a slight problem with this setup. These servers, which are supposed to be intimately connected to each other, have no idea that the others exist or that they are even config servers. This is fine—we're going to hook them up in a moment.

 Sometimes, people assume that they have to set up replication on config servers. Configuration servers do not use the same replication mechanism as "normal" *mongod* replication and should not be started as replica sets or master-slave setups. Just start config servers as normal, unconnected *mongod*s.

When you start up your config servers, feel free to use any of the options listed under "General Options" when you run *mongod --help*, except for --keyFile and --auth. Sharding does not support authentication at the moment, although this should change midway-through 1.9.

It's not a particularly good idea to run it with --quiet because you want to be able to figure out what's going on if something goes wrong. Instead of --quiet, use --logpath <file> and --logappend to send the logs somewhere so you'll have them if you run into problems.

The Sharding options apply to shards, not the configuration servers, so ignore those. You don't need to use any of the other options (under Replication, Replica set, or Master/slave) because you didn't start up your config servers with replication, right?

mongos

The next step is starting up a *mongos*. A sharded setup needs at least one *mongos* but can have as many as you'd like. Keep in mind that you will have to (or at least should) monitor all of the *mongos* processes you spin up, so you probably don't want thousands, but one *mongos* per application server usually is a good number. So, we'll log on to our application server and start up our first *mongos*.

```
$ ssh ny-02
ny-01$ mongos --configdb ny-01,sf-01,moon-01
```

Press Enter, and now all the config servers know about each other. The *mongos* is like the host of the party that introduces them all to each other.

You now have a trivial cluster. You can't actually store any data in it (configuration servers only store configuration, not data), but other than that, it's totally functional.

As you might want to use your database to read or write data, let's add some data storage.

Shards

All administration on a cluster is done through the *mongos*. So, connect your shell to the *mongos* process you started.

```
$ mongo ny-02:27017/admin
MongoDB shell version: 1.7.5
connecting to: admin
>
```

Make sure you're using the *admin* database. Setting up sharding requires commands to be run from the *admin* database.

Once you're connected, you can add a shard. There are two ways to add a shard, depending on whether the shard is a single server or a replica set. Let's say we have a single server, *sf-02*, that we've been using for data. We can make it the first shard by running the *addShard* command:

```
> db.runCommand({"addShard" : "sf-02:27017"})
{ "shardAdded" : "shard0000", "ok" : 1 }
```

This adds the server to the cluster. Now you can start storing and querying for data. (MongoDB will give you an error if you attempt to store data before you have any shards to put it on, for obvious reasons.)

In general, you should use a replica set, not a single server, for each shard. Replica sets will give you better availability. To add a replica set shard, you must give *addShard* a string of the form "setName/seed1[,seed2[,seed3[,...]]]". That is, you must give the set name and at least one member of the set (*mongos* can derive the other members as long as it can connect to someone).

For example, if we had a replica set creatively named replica set "rs" with members *rs1-a*, *rs1-b*, and *rs1-c*, we could say:

```
> db.runCommand({"addShard" : "rs/rs1-a,rs1-c"})
{ "shardAdded" : "rs", "ok" : 1 }
```

Notice that we ended up with a much nicer name this time! (I was the one who programmed it to pick up on the replica set name, so I'm particularly proud of it.) If you add a replica set, its name will become the shard name.

You can name a shard anything you want. If you don't want the default, use the name option when you add a shard.

```
> db.runCommand({"addShard" : "sf-02:27017", "name" : "Golden Gate shard"})
{ "shardAdded" : "Golden Gate shard", "ok" : 1 }
> db.runCommand({"addShard" : "set1/rs1-a,rs1-b", "name" : "replicaSet1"})
{ "shardAdded" : "replicaSet1", "ok" : 1 }
```

You'll have to refer to shards by name occasionally (see Chapter 5), so don't make the name too crazy or long.

Limiting shard size

By default, MongoDB will evenly distribute data between shards. This is useful if you're using a bunch of commodity servers, but you can run into problems if you have one gargantuan machine with 10 terabytes and one ho-hum machine with a few hundred gigabytes. If your servers are seriously out of balance, you should use the max Size option. This specifies the maximum size, in megabytes, that you want the shard to grow to.

Keep in mind that maxSize is more of a guideline than a rule. MongoDB will not cap off a shard at maxSize and not let it grow another byte, but rather it'll stop moving data to the shard and possibly move some data off. If it feels like it. So aim a bit low here.

maxSize is another option for the *addShard* command, so if you want to set a shard to only use 20GB, you could say:

```
> db.runCommand({"addShard" : "sfo/server1,server2", "maxSize" : 20000})
```

In the future, MongoDB will automatically figure out how much space it has to work with on each shard and plan accordingly. In the meantime, use maxSize to give it a hint.

Now you have a fully armed and operational cluster!

Databases and Collections

If you want MongoDB to distribute your data, you have to let it know which databases and collections you want to distribute. Start with the database. You have to tell MongoDB that a database can contain sharded collections before you try to shard its collections.

Let's say we're writing a blog application, so all of our collections live in the *blog* database. We can enable sharding on it with the command:

```
> db.adminCommand({"enableSharding" : "blog"})
{ "ok" : 1 }
```

Now we can shard a collection. To shard a collection, you must specify the collection and shard key. Suppose we were sharding on {"date" : 1, "author" : 1}.

```
> db.adminCommand({"shardCollection" : "blog.posts", key : {"date" : 1, "author" : 1}})
{ "collectionSharded" : "blog.posts", "ok" : 1 }
```

Note that we include the database name: *blog.posts*, not *posts*.

Sharding an Existing Collection

Sharding a collection is basically the same as sharding an empty collection, but it can take longer (and be more nerve-wracking), so here's what to expect.

Preparing Your Collection for Sharding

You must have an index on the shard key before you run the *shardcollection* command. If you shard an empty collection, MongoDB will create this index for you automatically, but you need to create the index manually if the collection already exists. Also, all documents must have a value for the shard key (and the value cannot be `null`).

shardcollection will return an error if you forget to index the shard key or the shard key is missing from certain documents. If you get an error, fix the cause and run *shardcollection* again.

After you've sharded the collection, you can insert documents with a `null`, although not missing, value in the shard key field.

Running *shardcollection*

Sharding an existing collection is (usually) not instantaneous. *shardcollection*'s job is to split your collection into chunks. As MongoDB doesn't keep any metadata about the size and shape of individual documents, *shardcollection* must look through your entire collection. The length of time this command takes depends on how many documents are in the collection, so a collection with fewer large documents can take much less time than a collection with many smaller documents, even if the on-disk size of the first collection is greater.

To get an upper bound on the time *shardcollection* will take to run, you can do covered index query (1.7.5+) on the shard key. A covered index query only touches the index, not the documents themselves, so you would do something like `db.collectionToSh ard.find({}, {key : 1, _id : 0})`, if *key* was your shard key.

shardcollection does not return control to the shell before it finishes sharding the collection (or errors out). Some people get worried because it looks like their shell or database has hung, but do not kill the command or the shell (or the database). If *shardcollection* hasn't returned yet, it isn't done; it'll return an error if there's a problem.

Plan to run this command at a time when not much else is going on. Certain parts of *shardcollection* do not yield very regularly, so other applications using the database may drag a bit. Also, *shardcollection* pulls the shard key index into memory which is likely to slow down your application as it has to hit disk more.

When you run *shardcollection*, the *mongos* process' log and the shard's log are the places to find information about what's going on. Start by looking at *mongos* log. You won't see any messages related to sharding at first, *shardcollection* does some preprocessing before it prints anything. This is probably the most nerve-wracking part of the process: you can't see any indication that *shardcollection* has started and reads and writes will block while this processing takes place. Stick with it, eventually you'll see something like:

```
CMD: shardcollection: { shardcollection: ns, key : sharkKey }
enable sharding on: ns with shard key: shardKey
about to create first chunk for: ns
successfully created first chunk for ns:ns at:primaryShard:server lastmod: 1|0
    min: { shardKey : MinKey } max : { shardKey : MaxKey }
```

This is the point where it has to look through the data to figure out where to chunk things. This can take a while.

If you look in the shard's log (not *mongos'*), you'll see:

```
request split points lookup for chunk ns { : MinKey } -->> { : MaxKey }
```

When it has finished finding split points, you may see a warning.

```
warning: Finding the split vector for ns over shardKey
    keyCount: num numSplits: num lookedAt: num took longTimems
```

This warning is totally ignorable, it's just telling you what you already knew: finding the split points took a long time. If you don't have a lot of documents, you might not see this warning.

Now it'll show you a list of all of the split points you chose, something like:

```
received splitChunk request: { splitChunk: ns, keyPattern: shardKey,
    min : { key: MinKey }, max : { key: MaxKey }, from : server,
    splitKeys: [ { key: key1 }, { key: key2 }, ... { key: keyN } ] }
```

There may be thousands of split keys listed, depending on how much data is in your collection. You probably won't notice this message, though, as the shard's log will immediately start filling up with lots of chunk splits. When it has finished creating all of the chunks, *shardcollection* will return { "collectionSharded" : *ns* , "ok" : 1 } in the shell. Your cluster should have normal response times to reads and writes again.

If a couple dozen chunks or more were created and you have more than one shard set up, MongoDB will immediately start balancing. Initial balancing of a chunk may take several hours, depending on the size of the data, but it should not seriously affect normal traffic.

For Large Data Sets

If you have more than approximately 256GB of data, *shardcollection* will successfully shard your collection, but it will not divide your collection into multiple chunks. It will leave it as one large chunk. (This limit was 25GB in 1.6 and briefly swung down to 8GB in 1.7 and is now a slightly more useful 256GB for 1.8.) This can be irritating when sharding a large collection, because you must wait while *shardcollection* chugs through millions of documents that you know it is going to end up refusing to chunk.

When it finishes, you'll see a message in the shard's log that looks like:

```
couldn't chunk recently created collection: ns 13333 can't split a chunk in that many parts
```

If this happens to you, don't panic. If *shardcollection* returned { "collectionSharded" : *ns* , "ok" : 1 }, your collection was successfully sharded, it's just all in one giant chunk. MongoDB will sort this out automatically: *shardcollection* won't divide things, but normal inserts and updates will trigger chunk splits.

As you continue to add data, MongoDB will divide your single large chunk into many chunks and then move those chunks around. *mongos* checks if it needs to split anything after about a dozen megabytes of new data is inserted. If your application inserts data and you just let it do it's thing, *mongos* will start splitting the chunk.

Note that, if *shardcollection* leaves your data in one chunk, the balancer will not kick in immediately, or it may kick in and not do much as chunks get split to more reasonable sizes. This is not a huge problem for most systems (unless you're about to run out of disk space), it just means the initial splitting and migrating process takes longer.

In future releases, *shardcollection* will be able to split collections into multiple chunks regardless of size (vote for and/or watch SERVER-2271 (*http://jira.mongodb.org/ browse/SERVER-2271*)).

Adding and Removing Capacity

As your application continues to grow, you'll need to add more shards. When you add a shard, MongoDB will start moving data from the existing shards to the new one. Keep in mind that moving data puts added pressure on shards. MongoDB tries to do this as gently as possible; it slowly moves one chunk at a time, then tries again later if the server seems busy. However, no matter how delicately MongoDB does it, moving chunks adds load.

This means that if you wait until your cluster is running at capacity to add more shards, adding a new shard can bring your application to a grinding halt through a chain re-action. Say your existing shards are just about maxed out, so you bring up a new shard to help with the load. The balancer pokes Shard 1 and asks it to send a chunk to the new shard. Shard 1 has just enough memory to keep your application's working set of data in RAM, and now it's going to have to pull a whole chunk into memory. The data that your application is using starts getting shunted out of RAM to make room for the chunk. This means that your application starts having to do disk seeks and MongoDB is doing disk seeks for chunk data. As queries start taking longer, requests begin to pile up, exacerbating the problem (see Figure 3-2).

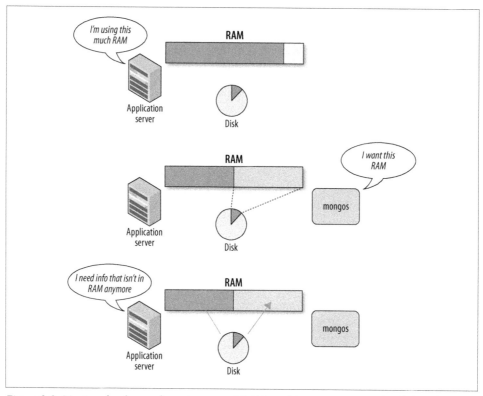

Figure 3-2. Moving chunks can force data out of RAM, making more requests hit disk and slowing everything down

The lesson? Add shards while you still have room to maneuver. If you no longer have that room, add shards in the middle of the night (or at another non-busy time). If you don't have a non-busy time and you waited too long, there are a couple of ways to hack around it, but they are neither fun nor easy. (You can manually create a Frankenstein shard from backups of your existing shard, manually change the *config.chunks* collection, and restart your whole cluster—this is obviously not recommended.) Add shards early and often.

So! How do you add shards? The same way that you added the first shard above, with the *addShard* command.

One interesting thing about adding subsequent shards is that they don't have to be empty. They cannot have databases that already exist in the cluster, but if your cluster has a *foo* database and you add a shard with a *bar* database, that's fine, as the config servers will pick up on it and it'll pop up in cluster info. Therefore, if you want, you can bring together a couple different systems into one large, sharded cluster.

Removing Shards

Sometimes removing shards comes up. Someone might shard too early or they realize that they chose the wrong shard key, so they want to get everything back onto one shard, dump, restore, and try again. You might just want to take certain servers offline.

The *removeShard* command lets you take a shard out of the cluster.

```
> db.runCommand({removeShard : "Golden Gate shard"})
{
    "msg" : "draining started successfully",
    "state" : "started",
    "shard" : "Golden Gate shard",
    "ok" : 1
}
```

Note that the message says "started successfully." It has to move all of the information that was on this shard to other shards before it can remove this shard. As mentioned above, moving data from shard to shard is pretty slow. The *removeShard* command returns immediately, and you must poll it to find out if it has finished. If you call it again, you'll see something like:

```
> db.runCommand({removeShard : "Golden Gate shard"})
{
    "msg" : "draining ongoing",
    "state" : "ongoing",
    "remaining" : {
        "chunks" : NumberLong(2),
        "dbs" : NumberLong(1)
    },
    "ok" : 1
}
```

Once it's done, its status will change to "completed." Then, you can safely shut down the shard (or use it as a non-sharded MongoDB server).

```
> db.runCommand({removeShard : "Golden Gate shard"})
{
    "msg" : "removeshard completed successfully",
    "state" : "completed",
    "shard" : "Golden Gate shard",
    "ok" : 1
}
```

This means that shard has been completely drained and may be shut down or used for other purposes.

Changing Servers in a Shard

If you're using a replica set, you can add or remove servers from the replica set and your *mongos* will pick up on the change. To modify your replica set in a cluster, do the exact same thing you would do if it was running independently: connect to the primary (*not* through *mongos*) and make any configuration changes you need.

CHAPTER 4

Working With a Cluster

Querying a MongoDB cluster is usually identical to querying a single *mongod*. However, there are some exceptions that are worth knowing about.

Querying

If you are using replica sets as shards and a *mongos* version 1.7.4 or more recent, you can distribute reads to slaves in a cluster. This can be handy for handling read load, although the usual caveats on querying slaves apply: you must be willing to get older data.

To query a slave through *mongos*, you must set the "slave okay" option (basically checking off that you're okay with getting possibly out-of-date data) with whatever driver you're using. In the shell, this looks like:

```
> db.getMongo().setSlaveOk()
```

Then query the *mongos* normally.

"Why Am I Getting This?"

When you work with a cluster, you lose the ability to examine an entire collection as a single "snapshot in time." Many people don't realize the ramifications of this until it hits them in the nose, so we'll go over some of the common ways it can affect applications.

Counting

When you do a *count* on a sharded collection, you may not get the results you expect. You may get quite a few more documents than actually exist.

The way a *count* works is the *mongos* forwards the count command to every shard in the cluster. Then, each shard does a count and sends its results back to the *mongos*, which totals them up and sends them to the user. If there is a migration occurring, many documents can be present (and thus counted) on more than one shard.

When MongoDB migrates a chunk, it starts copying it from one shard to another. It still routes all reads and writes to that chunk to the old shard, but it is gradually being populated on the other shard. Once the chunk has finished "moving," it actually exists on both shards. As the final step, MongoDB updates the config servers and deletes the copy of the data from the original shard (see Figure 4-1).

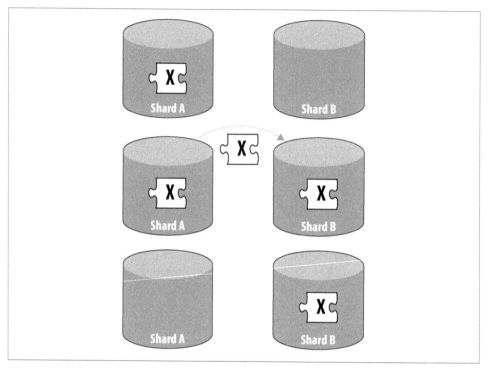

Figure 4-1. A chunk is migrated by copying it to the new shard, then deleting it from the shard it came from

Thus, when data is counted, it ends up getting counted twice. MongoDB may hack around this in the future, but for now, keep in mind that counts may overshoot the actual number of documents.

Unique Indexes

Suppose we were sharding on *email* and wanted to have a unique index on *username*. This is not possible to enforce with a cluster.

Let's say we have two application servers processing users. One application server adds a new user document with the following fields:

```
{
    "_id" : ObjectId("4d2a2e9f74de15b8306fe7d0"),
    "username" : "andrew",
    "email" : "awesome.guy@example.com"
}
```

The only way to check that "andrew" is the only "andrew" in the cluster is to go through every username entry on every machine. Let's say MongoDB goes through all the shards and no one else has an "andrew" username, so it's just about to write the document on Shard 3 when the second appserver sends this document to be inserted:

```
{
    "_id" : ObjectId("4d2a2f7c56d1bb09196fe7d0"),
    "username" : "andrew",
    "email" : "cool.guy@example.com"
}
```

Once again, every shard checks that it has no users with username "andrew". They still don't because the first document hasn't been written yet, so Shard 1 goes ahead and writes this document. Then Shard 3 finally gets around to writing the first document. Now there are two people with the same username!

The only way to guarantee no duplicates between shards in the general case is to lock down the entire cluster every time you do a write until the write has been confirmed successful. This is not performant for a system with a decent rate of writes.

Therefore, you cannot guarantee uniqueness on any key other than the shard key. You can guarantee uniqueness on the shard key because a given document can only go to one chunk, so it only has to be unique on that one shard, and it'll be guaranteed unique in the whole cluster. You can also have a unique index that is prefixed by the shard key. For example, if we sharded the users collection on *username*, as above, but with the unique option, we could create a unique index on {username : 1, email : 1}.

One interesting consequence of this is that, unless you're sharding on *_id*, you can create non-unique *_id*s. This isn't recommended (and it can get you into trouble if chunks move), but it is possible.

Updating

Updates, by default, only update a single record. This means that they run into the same problem unique indexes do: there's no good way of guaranteeing that something happens once across multiple shards. If you're doing a single-document update, it must use the shard key in the criteria (update's first argument). If you do not, you'll get an error.

```
> db.adminCommand({shardCollection : "test.x", key : {"y" : 1}})
{ "shardedCollection" : "test.x", "ok" : 1 }
>
> // works okay
> db.x.update({y : 1}, {$set : {z : 2}}, true)
>
```

```
> // error
> db.x.update({z : 2}, {$set : {w : 4}})
can't do non-multi update with query that doesn't have the shard key
```

You can do a multiupdate using any criteria you want.

```
> db.x.update({z : 2}, {$set : {w : 4}}, false, true)
> // no error
```

If you run across an odd error message, consider whether the operation you're trying to perform would have to atomically look at the entire cluster. Such operations are not allowed.

MapReduce

When you run a MapReduce on a cluster, each shard performs its own map and reduce. *mongos* chooses a "leader" shard and sends all the reduced data from the other shards to that one for a final reduce. Once the data is reduced to its final form, it will be output in whatever method you've specified.

As sharding splits the job across multiple machines, it can perform MapReduces faster than a single server. However, it still isn't meant for real-time calculations.

Temporary Collections

In 1.6, MapReduce created temporary collections unless you specified the "out" option. These temporary collections were dropped when the connection that created them was closed. This worked well on a single server, but *mongos* keeps its own connection pools and never closes connections to shards. Thus, temporary collections were never cleaned up (because the connection that created them never closed), and they would just hang around forever, growing more and more numerous.

If you're running 1.6 and doing MapReduces, you'll have to manually clean up your temporary collections. You can run the following function to delete all of the temporary collections in a given database:

```
var dropTempCollections = function(dbName) {
    var target = db.getSisterDB(dbName);
    var names = target.getCollectionNames();

    for (var i = 0; i < names.length; i++) {
        if (names[i].match(/tmp\.mr\./)){
            target[names[i]].drop();
        }
    }
}
```

In later versions, MapReduce forces you to choose to do something with your output. See the documentation (*http://www.mongodb.org/display/DOCS/MapReduce*) for details.

CHAPTER 5

Administration

Whereas the last chapter covered working with MongoDB from an application developer's standpoint, this chapter covers some more operational aspects of running a cluster. Once you have a cluster up and running, how do you know what's going on?

Using the Shell

As with a single instance of MongoDB, most administration on a cluster can be done through the *mongo* shell.

Getting a Summary

db.printShardingStatus() is your executive summary. It gathers all the important information about your cluster and presents it nicely for you.

```
> db.printShardingStatus()
--- Sharding Status ---
sharding version: { "_id" : 1, "version" : 3 }
shards:
{ "_id" : "shard0000", "host" : "ubuntu:27017" }
{ "_id" : "shard0001", "host" : "ubuntu:27018" }
databases:
{ "_id" : "admin", "partitioned" : false, "primary" : "config" }
{ "_id" : "test", "partitioned" : true, "primary" : "shard0000" }
test.foo chunks:
shard0001 15
shard0000 16
{ "_id" : { $minKey : 1 } } -->> { "_id" : 0 } on : shard1 { "t" : 2, "i" : 0 }
{ "_id" : 0 } -->> { "_id" : 15074 } on : shard1 { "t" : 3, "i" : 0 }
{ "_id" : 15074 } -->> { "_id" : 30282 } on : shard1 { "t" : 4, "i" : 0 }
{ "_id" : 30282 } -->> { "_id" : 44946 } on : shard1 { "t" : 5, "i" : 0 }
{ "_id" : 44946 } -->> { "_id" : 59467 } on : shard1 { "t" : 7, "i" : 0 }
{ "_id" : 59467 } -->> { "_id" : 73838 } on : shard1 { "t" : 8, "i" : 0 }
... some lines omitted ...
{ "_id" : 412949 } -->> { "_id" : 426349 } on : shard1 { "t" : 6, "i" : 4 }
{ "_id" : 426349 } -->> { "_id" : 457636 } on : shard1 { "t" : 7, "i" : 2 }
```

```
37
{ "_id" : 457636 } -->> { "_id" : 471683 } on : shard1 { "t" : 7, "i" : 4 }
{ "_id" : 471683 } -->> { "_id" : 486547 } on : shard1 { "t" : 7, "i" : 6 }
{ "_id" : 486547 } -->> { "_id" : { $maxKey : 1 } } on : shard1 { "t" : 7, "i" : 7 }
```

db.printShardingStatus() prints a list of all of your shards and databases. Each sharded collection has an entry (there's only one sharded collection here, *test.foo*). It shows you how chunks are distributed (15 chunks on shard0001 and 16 chunks on shard0000). Then it gives detailed information about each chunk: its range—e.g., { "_id" : 115882 } -->> { "_id" : 130403 } corresponding to *_id*s in *[115882, 130403)*—and what shard it's on. It also gives the major and minor version of the chunk, which you don't have to worry about.

Each database created has a primary shard that is its "home base." In this case, the *test* database was randomly assigned shard0000 as its home. This doesn't really mean anything—shard0001 ended up with more chunks than shard0000! This field should never matter to you, so you can ignore it. If you remove a shard and some database has its "home" there, that database's home will automatically be moved to a shard that's still in the cluster.

db.printShardingStatus() can get really long when you have a big collection, as it lists every chunk on every shard. If you have a large cluster, you can dive in and get more precise information, but this is a good, simple overview when you're starting out.

The config Collections

mongos forward your requests to the appropriate shard—except for when you query the *config* database. Accessing the *config* database patches you through to the config servers, and it is where you can find all the cluster's configuration information. If you do have a collection with hundreds or thousands of chunks, it's worth it to learn about the contents of the *config* database so you can query for specific info, instead of getting a summary of your entire setup.

Let's take a look at the *config* database. Assuming you have a cluster set up, you should see these collections:

```
> use config
switched to db config
> show collections
changelog
chunks
collections
databases
lockpings
locks
mongos
settings
shards
system.indexes
version
```

Many of the collections are just accounting for what's in the cluster:

config.mongos

A list of all *mongos* processes, past and present

```
> db.mongos.find()
{ "_id" : "ubuntu:10000", "ping" : ISODate("2011-01-08T10:11:23"), "up" : 0 }
{ "_id" : "ubuntu:10000", "ping" : ISODate("2011-01-08T10:11:23"), "up" : 20 }
{ "_id" : "ubuntu:10000", "ping" : ISODate("2011-01-08T10:11:23"), "up" : 1 }
```

_id is the hostname of the *mongos*. *ping* is the last time the config server pinged it. *up* is whether it thinks the *mongos* is up or not. If you bring up a *mongos*, even if it's just for a few seconds, it will be added to this list and will never disappear. It doesn't really matter, it's not like you're going to be bringing up millions of *mongos* servers, but it's something to be aware of so you don't get confused if you look at the list.

config.shards

All the shards in the cluster

config.databases

All the databases, sharded and non-sharded

config.collections

All the sharded collections

config.chunks

All the chunks in the cluster

config.settings contains (theoretically) tweakable settings that depend on the database version. Currently, *config.settings* allows you to change the chunk size (but don't!) and turn off the balancer, which you usually shouldn't need to do. You can change these settings by running an update. For example, to turn off the balancer:

```
> db.settings.update({"_id" : "balancer"}, {"$set" : {"stopped" : true }}, true)
```

If it's in the middle of a balancing round, it won't turn off until the current balancing has finished.

The only other collection that might be of interest is the *config.changelog* collection. It is a *very* detailed log of every split and migrate that happens. You can use it to retrace the steps that got your cluster to whatever its current configuration is. Usually it is more detail than you need, though.

"I Want to Do X, Who Do I Connect To?"

If you want to do any sort of normal reads, writes, or administration, the answer is always "a *mongos*." It can be any *mongos* (remember that they're stateless), but it's always a *mongos*—not a shard, not a config server.

You might connect to a config server or a shard if you're trying to do something unusual. This might be looking at a shard's data directly or manually editing a messed up configuration. For example, you'll have to connect directly to a shard to change a replica set configuration.

Remember that config servers and shards are just normal *mongod*s; anything you know how to do on a *mongod* you can do on a config server or shard. However, in the normal course of operation, you should almost never have to connect to them. All normal operations should go through *mongos*.

Monitoring

Monitoring is crucially important when you have a cluster. All of the advice for monitoring a single node applies when monitoring many nodes, so make sure you have read the documentation on monitoring (*http://www.mongodb.org/display/DOCS/Monitoring+and+Diagnostics*).

Don't forget that your network becomes more of a factor when you have multiple machines. If a server says that it can't reach another server, investigate the possibility that the network between two has gone down.

If possible, leave a shell connected to your cluster. Making a connection requires MongoDB to briefly give the connection a lock, which can be a problem for debugging. Say a server is acting funny, so you fire up a shell to look at it. Unfortunately, the *mongod* is stuck in a write lock, so the shell will sit there forever trying to acquire the lock and never finish connecting. To be on the safe side, leave a shell open.

mongostat

mongostat is the most comprehensive monitoring available. It gives you tons of information about what's going on with a server, from load to page faulting to number of connections open.

If you're running a cluster, you can start up a separate *mongostat* for every server, but you can also run *mongostat --discover* on a *mongos* and it will figure out every member of the cluster and display their stats.

For example, if we start up a cluster using the *simple-setup.py* script described in Chapter 4, it will find all the *mongos* processes and all of the shards:

```
$ mongostat --discover
                 mapped  vsize   res faults locked % idx miss %  conn      time repl
localhost:27017     0m   105m    3m      0        0          0      2  22:59:50  RTR
localhost:30001    80m   175m    5m      0        0          0      3  22:59:50
localhost:30002     0m    95m    5m      0        0          0      3  22:59:50
localhost:30003     0m    95m    5m      0        0          0      3  22:59:50

localhost:27017     0m   105m    3m      0        0          0      2  22:59:51  RTR
localhost:30001    80m   175m    5m      0        0          0      3  22:59:51
localhost:30002     0m    95m    5m      0        0          0      3  22:59:51
localhost:30003     0m    95m    5m      0        0          0      3  22:59:51
```

I've simplified the output and removed a number of columns because I'm limited to 80 characters per line and *mongostat* goes a good 166 characters wide. Also, the spacing is a little funky because the tool starts with "normal" *mongostat* spacing, figures out what the rest of the cluster is, and adds a couple more fields: *qr|qw* and *ar|aw*. These fields show how many connections are queued for reads and writes and how many are actively reading and writing.

The Web Admin Interface

If you're using replica sets for shards, make sure you start them with the `--rest` option. The web admin interface for replica sets (*http://localhost:28017/_replSet*, if *mongod* is running on port 27017) gives you loads of information.

Backups

Taking backups on a running cluster turns out to be a difficult problem. Data is constantly being added and removed by the application, as usual, but it's also being moved around by the balancer. If you take a dump of a shard today and restore it tomorrow, you may have the same documents in two places or end up missing some documents altogether (see Figure 5-1).

The problem with taking backups is that you usually only want to restore parts of your cluster (you don't want to restore the entire cluster from yesterday's backup, just the node that went down). If you restore data from a backup, you have to be careful. Look at the config servers and see which chunks are supposed to be on the shard you're restoring. Then only restore data from those chunks using your backups (and *mongorestore*).

If you want a snapshot of the whole cluster, you would have to turn off the balancer, *fsync* and lock the slaves in the cluster, take dumps from them, then unlock them and restart the balancer. Typically people just take backups from individual shards.

Config Server Backups

If you have three config servers, shut one of them down and copy its files to a backup location. As two config servers are still running, your cluster configuration will be read-only, but everything else should operate normally. Backing up data from a config server should only take a few minutes: even the largest installs generate less than a gigabyte of config data.

If you have a single config server and you're using that single config server in production, it becomes a little trickier (please don't use a single config server in production). You should do a targetted query through each of the *mongos* processes running to ensure that they all have up-to-date versions of the configuration. Once you've done that, bring down the config server and make a backup of its files.

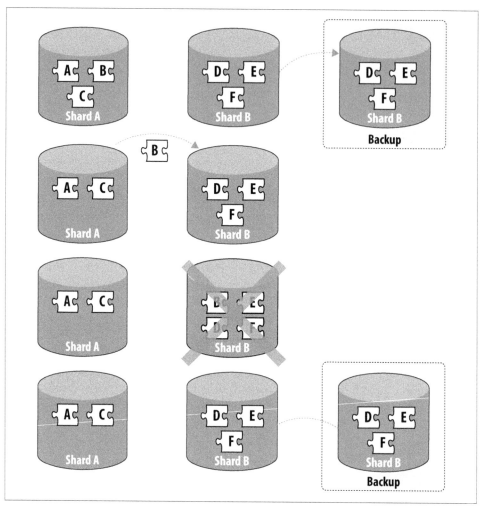

Figure 5-1. Here, a backup is taken before a migrate. If the shard crashes after the migrate is complete and restored from backup, the cluster will be missing the migrated chunk.

Suggestions on Architecture

You can create a sharded cluster and leave it at that, but what happens when you want to do routine maintenance? There are a few extra pieces you can add that will make your setup easier to manage.

Create an Emergency Site

The name implies that you're running a website, but this applies to most types of application. If you need to bring your application down occasionally (e.g., to do maintenance, roll out changes, or in an emergency), it's very handy to have an emergency site that you can switch over to.

The emergency site should not use your cluster at all. If it uses a database, it should be completely disconnected from your main database. You could also have it serve data from a cache or be a completely static site, depending on your application. It's a good idea to set up something for users to look at, though, other than an Apache error page.

Create a Moat

A excellent way to prevent or minimize all sorts of problems is to create a virtual moat around your machines and control access to the cluster via a queue.

A queue can allow your application to continue handling writes in a planned outage, or at least prevent any writes that didn't quite make it before the outage from getting lost. You can keep them on the queue until MongoDB is up again and then send them to the *mongos*.

A queue isn't only useful for disasters—it can also be helpful in regulating bursty traffic. A queue can hold the burst and release a nice, constant stream of requests, instead of allowing a sudden flood to swamp the cluster. You can also use a queue going the other way: to cache results coming out of MongoDB.

There are lots of different queues you could use: Amazon's SQS, RabbitMQ, or even a MongoDB capped collection (although make sure it's on a separate server than the cluster it's protecting). Use whatever queue you're comfortable with.

Queues won't work for all applications. For example, they don't work with applications that need real-time data. However, if you have an application that can stand small delays, a queue can be useful intermediary between the world and your database.

What to Do When Things Go Wrong

As mentioned in the first chapter, network partitions, server crashes, and other problems can cause a whole variety of issues. MongoDB can "self-heal," at least temporarily, from many of these issues. This section covers which outages you can sleep through and which ones you can't, as well as preparing your application to deal with outages.

A Shard Goes Down

If an entire shard goes down, reads and writes that would have hit that shard will return errors. Your application should handle those errors (it'll be whatever your language's equivalent of an exception is, thrown as you iterated through a cursor). For example, if the first three results for some query were on the shard that is up and the next shard containing useful chunks is down, you'd get something like:

```
> db.foo.find()
{ "_id" : 1 }
{ "_id" : 2 }
{ "_id" : 3 }
error: mongos connectionpool:
connect failed ny-01:10000 : couldn't connect to server ny-01:10000
```

Be prepared to handle this error and keep going gracefully. Depending on your application, you could also do exclusively targeted queries until the shard comes back online.

In 1.7.5 and later, you can set a "partial results" flag when you send a query to *mongos*. If this flag is set (it defaults to unset), *mongos* will only return results from shards that are up and not return any errors.

Most of a Shard Is Down

If you are using replica sets for shards, hopefully an entire shard won't go down, but merely a server or two in the set. If the set loses a majority of its members, no one will be able to become master (without manual rejiggering), and so the set will be read-only. If a set becomes read-only, make sure your application is only sending it reads and using slaveOkay.

If you're using replica sets, hopefully a single server (or even a few servers) failing won't affect your application at all. The other servers in the set will pick up the slack and your application won't even notice the change.

 In 1.6, if a replica set configuration changes, there may be a zillion identical messages printed to the log. Every connection between *mongos* and the shard prints a message when it notices that its replica set connection is out-of-date and updates it. However, it shouldn't have an impact on what's actually happening—it's just a lot of sound and fury. This has been fixed for 1.8; *mongos* is much smarter about updating replica set configurations.

Config Servers Going Down

If a config server goes down, there will be no immediate impact on cluster performance, but no configuration changes can be made. All the config servers work in concert, so none of the other config servers can make any changes while even a single of their brethren have fallen. The thing to note about config servers is that no configuration can change while a config server is down—you can't add mongos servers, you can't migrate data, you can't add or remove databases or collections, and you can't change replica set configurations.

If a config server crashes, do get it back up so that your config can change when it needs to, but it shouldn't affect the immediate operation of your cluster at all. Make sure you monitor config servers and, if one fails, get it right back up.

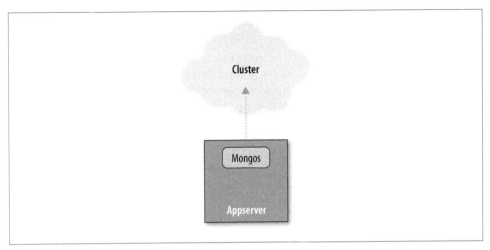

Figure 5-2. An appserver running a mongos.

Having a config server go down can put some pressure on your servers if there is a migrate in progress. One of the last steps of the migrate is to update the config servers. Because one server is down, they can't be updated, so the shards will have to back out the migration and delete all the data they just painstakingly copied. If your shards aren't overloaded, this shouldn't be too painful, but it is a bit of a waste.

Mongos Processes Going Down

As you can always have extra *mongos* processes and they have no state, it's not too big a deal if one goes down. The recommended setup is to run one *mongos* on each appserver and have each appserver talk to its local *mongos* (Figure 5-2). Then, if the whole machine goes down, no one is trying to talk to a *mongos* that isn't there.

Have a couple extra *mongos* servers out there that you can fail over to if one *mongos* process crashes while the application server is still okay. Most drivers let you specify a list of servers to connect to and will try them in order. So, you could specify your preferred *mongos* first, then your backup *mongos*. If one goes down, your application can handle the exception (in whatever language you're using) and the driver will automatically shunt the application over to your backup *mongos* for the next request.

You can also just try restarting a crashed *mongos* if the machine is okay, as they are stateless and store no data.

Other Considerations

Each of the points above is handled in isolation from anything else that could go wrong. Sometimes, if you have a network partition, you might lose entire shards, parts of other shards, config servers, and mongos processes. You should think carefully about how to handle various scenarios from both user-facing (will users still be able to do anything?) and application-design (will the application still do something sensible?) perspectives.

Finally, MongoDB tries to let a lot go wrong before exposing a loss of functionality. If you have the perfect storm (and you will), you'll lose functionality, but day-to-day server crashes, power outages, and network partitions shouldn't cause huge problems. Keep an eye on your monitoring and don't panic.

CHAPTER 6

Further Reading

If you follow the advice in the preceding chapters, you should be well on your way to an efficient and predictable distributed system that can grow as you need. If you have further questions or are confused about anything, feel free to email me at *kristina@10gen.com.*

If you're interested in learning more about sharding, there are quite a few resources available:

- The MongoDB wiki has a large section on sharding (*http://www.mongodb.org/display/DOCS/Sharding*), with everything from configuration examples to discussions of internals.
- The MongoDB user list (*http://groups.google.com/group/mongodb-user*) is a great place to ask questions.
- There are lots of useful little pieces of code in the mongo-snippets (*https://github.com/mongodb/mongo-snippets*) repository.
- Boxed Ice runs a production MongoDB cluster and often writes useful articles in their blog (*http://blog.boxedice.com/mongodb/*) about running MongoDB.
- If you're interested in reading more about distributed computing theory, I highly recommend Leslie Lamport's original Paxos paper (*http://research.microsoft.com/en-us/um/people/lamport/pubs/lamport-paxos.pdf*), which is an entertaining and instructive read.

Also, if you enjoyed this, I write a blog (*http://www.snailinaturtleneck.com*) that mostly covers advanced MongoDB topics.

Get even more for your money.

Join the O'Reilly Community, and register the O'Reilly books you own. It's free, and you'll get:

- $4.99 ebook upgrade offer
- 40% upgrade offer on O'Reilly print books
- Membership discounts on books and events
- Free lifetime updates to ebooks and videos
- Multiple ebook formats, DRM FREE
- Participation in the O'Reilly community
- Newsletters
- Account management
- 100% Satisfaction Guarantee

Signing up is easy:

1. **Go to: oreilly.com/go/register**
2. **Create an O'Reilly login.**
3. **Provide your address.**
4. **Register your books.**

Note: English-language books only

To order books online:
oreilly.com/store

For questions about products or an order:
orders@oreilly.com

To sign up to get topic-specific email announcements and/or news about upcoming books, conferences, special offers, and new technologies:
elists@oreilly.com

For technical questions about book content:
booktech@oreilly.com

To submit new book proposals to our editors:
proposals@oreilly.com

O'Reilly books are available in multiple DRM-free ebook formats. For more information:
oreilly.com/ebooks

O'REILLY®

Spreading the knowledge of innovators | oreilly.com

The information you need, when and where you need it.

With Safari Books Online, you can:

Access the contents of thousands of technology and business books

- Quickly search over 7000 books and certification guides
- Download whole books or chapters in PDF format, at no extra cost, to print or read on the go
- Copy and paste code
- Save up to 35% on O'Reilly print books
- **New!** Access mobile-friendly books directly from cell phones and mobile devices

Stay up-to-date on emerging topics before the books are published

- Get on-demand access to evolving manuscripts.
- Interact directly with authors of upcoming books

Explore thousands of hours of video on technology and design topics

- Learn from expert video tutorials
- Watch and replay recorded conference sessions

Milton Keynes UK
Ingram Content Group UK Ltd.
UKHW012036270824
447508UK00009B/195